Foreseeable Futures

By William Matthews

Ruining the New Road
Sleek for the Long Flight
Sticks & Stones
Rising and Falling
Flood
A Happy Childhood

Houghton Mifflin Company

Boston 1987

Foreseeable Futures

POEMS BY

William Matthews

Library of Congress Cataloging-in-Publication Data

Matthews, William, date.
    Foreseeable futures.

    I. Title.
PS3563.A855F6   1987   811'.54   86-21400
ISBN 0-395-43099-2
ISBN 0-395-43100-X (pbk.)

Printed in the United States of America

Q 10 9 8 7 6 5 4 3 2 1

The poems in this book have appeared in the following
magazines: *The Atlantic Monthly:* "Herd of Buffalo
Crossing the Missouri on Ice." *Black Warrior Review:*
"Orthopedic Surgery Ward." *Brooklyn Review:*
"Attention, Shoppers." *Chiaroscuro:* "Dog Life"; "Photo
of the Author with a Favorite Pig." *College English:*
"Writer-in-Residence." *Columbia:* "Search for the Perfect
Pasta." *Crazy Horse:* "Fellow Oddballs"; "Men in
Dark Suits." *Denver Quarterly:* "Mail Order Catalogs."
Domestic Crude: "Three Vacations," part 2. *Field:*
"Liver Cancer." *Georgia Review:* "Construction."
Hubbub: "Three Vacations," part 1. *Louisville Review:*
"Puberty." *New England Review and Bread Loaf
Quarterly:* "Black Box"; "Cabbage"; "Days Beyond
Recall"; "Torch Song." *The New Yorker:* "Minuscule
Things"; "Scenic View." *Ohio Review:* "Caddies'
Day, the Country Club, a Small Town in Ohio."
Partisan Review: "Leipzig, 1894." *Plainsong:* "Blue
Notes"; "By Heart"; "Hope"; "*Lucky* and *Unlucky*."
Ploughshares: "Schoolboys with Dog, Winter";
"Self-knowledge." *Quarterly West:* "Three
Vacations," part 3.

I would like to thank the National Endowment for the Arts and the Ingram Merrill Foundation for fellowships during which much of this book was written.

FOR ARLENE

An ascetic boasted to Buddha that he could walk on water. "How long did it take you to perfect this skill?" Buddha asked. "Ten years," replied the ascetic. "What a shame," said Buddha; "for a few coins you could have taken the ferry."

Contents

————————

Foreseeable Futures

Men in Dark Suits

Like talk overheard across water, they seem to have come
from far away louder and nearer than we thought, though
what we hear isn't what's said, but the blurred, rolling

surf of speech. They remind me of umpires trudging amiably
across the close-mown lawn — their burly ease, the way
the day seems not quite to have happened yet. The fervors

and dust, the long shadows, all these are still to come
and the men are drawing near. For all they seem at this
narrowing distance to be fathers roped together by banter,

won't we in our turn cross as familiarly the dwindling
field, ambling to low-voiced badinage about how like
them we've become, only to greet a cleric with a widow —

one of ours — crooked in his arm? But none
of this has happened yet. As steadily as afternoon
men come, joyless but content, across the ample grass.

Fellow Oddballs

The sodden sleep from which we open like umbrellas,
the way money keeps *us* in circulation, the scumbled lists
we make of what to do and what, God help us, to undo —

an oddball knows an oddball at forty or at 40,000
paces. Let's raise our dribble glasses. Here's to us,
morose at dances and giggly in committee,

and here's to us on whose ironic bodies new clothes
pucker that clung like shrink wrap to the manikins.
And here's to the threadbare charm of our self-pity.

For when the waiters, who are really actors between parts,
have crumbed for the last time our wobbly tables,
and we've patted our pockets for keys and cigarettes

enough until tomorrow, for the coat-check token
and for whatever's missing, well then, what next? God knows,
who counts us on God's shapely toes, one and one and one.

April in the Berkshires

———————

Dogs skulk, clouds moil and froth, humans
begin to cook — butter, a blue waver of flame,
chopped onions. A styptic rain stings grit and soot

from the noon air. Here and there, like the mess
after a party, pink smudgily tinges the bushes,
but they'll be long weeks of mud and sweaters

before a finch dips and percolates through
the backyard air like the talk of old friends.
It feels like the very middle, the exact

fulcrum of our lives. Our places wait for us
in the yard, like shadows furled in bud.
On the chill wands of the forsythia pale

yellow tatters wave. How long has Mr. Forsyth
been dead? Onto the lawn we go.
Lights, camera, action: the story of our lives.

———————

Photo of the Author with a Favorite Pig

Behind its snout like a huge button,
like an almost clean plate, the pig
looks candid compared to the author,

and why not? He has a way with words,
but the unspeakable pig, squat
and foursquare as a bathtub,

squints frankly. Nobody knows
the trouble it's seen, this rained-out
pork roast, this ham escaped into

its corpulent jokes, its body of work.
The author is skinny and looks serious:
what will he say next? The copious pig

has every appearance of knowing,
from his pert, coiled tail to the wispy tips
of his edible ears, but the pig isn't telling.

Toasts to the Rented House in Polgeto

Here's to the leafy gossip of the poplars,
and to the calm phone into which we pleaded
Pronto, pronto? Why were we so alarmed?

Here's to the antique Fiat tractor that clattered
late at night along the slope across the road,
and to its smoky headlight, and to the dark

which fell in folds on the raw soil in the tractor's
wake as it coughed and hawked and rattled home.
Here's to the cats that slept on the sun-sodden

terrace, and dreamed of what? Do pigs dream
of acorns, or sheep of company? In the umber
haze of summer the inquiline body is happy.

It cooks outdoors, naps, plows when it's cool.
Here's to the body, then, our only real estate,
our squander, our hoard. Long may it contend.

The Accompanist

———————

Don't play too much, don't play
too loud, don't play the melody.
You have to anticipate her
and to subdue yourself.
She used to give me her smoky
eye when I got boisterous,
so I learned to play on tip-
toe and to play the better half
of what I might. I don't like
to complain, though I notice
that I get around to it somehow.
We made a living and good music,
both, night after night, the blue
curlicues of smoke rubbing their
staling and wispy backs
against the ceilings, the flat
drinks and scarce taxis, the jazz life
we bitch about the way Army pals
complain about the food and then
re-up. Some people like to say
with smut in their voices how playing
the way we did at our best is partly
sexual. OK, I could tell them

———

a tale or two, and I've heard
the records Lester cut with Lady Day
and all that rap, and it's partly
sexual but it's mostly practice
and music. As for partly sexual,
I'll take wholly sexual any day,
but that's a duet and we're talking
accompaniment. Remember "Reckless
Blues"? Bessie Smith sings out "Daddy"
and Louis Armstrong plays back "Daddy"
as clear through his horn as if he'd
spoken it. But it's her daddy and her
story. When you play it you become
your part in it, one of her beautiful
troubles, and then, however much music
can do this, part of her consolation,
the way pain and joy eat off each other's
plates, but mostly you play to drunks,
to the night, to the way you judge
and pardon yourself, to all that goes
not unsung, but unrecorded.

———

7

Herd of Buffalo Crossing the Missouri on Ice

If dragonflies can mate atop the surface tension
of water, surely these tons of bison can mince
across the river, their fur peeling in strips like old

wallpaper, their huge eyes adjusting to how far
they can see when there's no big or little bluestem,
no Indian grass nor prairie cord grass to plod through.

Maybe because it's bright in the blown snow
and swirling grit, their vast heads are lowered
to the gray ice: nothing to eat, little to smell.

They have their own currents. You could watch a herd
of running pronghorn swerve like a river rounding
a meander and see better what I mean. But

bison are a deeper, deliberate water, and there will
never be enough water for any West but the one
into which we watch these bison carefully disappear.

Lucky *and* Unlucky

mean the same thing, like *flammable* and *inflammable*.
Four crows bicker on the peak of my roof, then three
rumple upward like charred paper lifting from a fire

with the malarial torpor of the poorest tropics.
But it's Seattle in February, and alder smoke
uncoils from the chimneys; it's Saturday:

errands and children, errands and loneliness.
Is the future the history of memory or forgetting?
The cleaners, the drugstore, the lumber yard . . .

At home the crow just sits there, the color of blue-
black ink still drying, each of its eyes as big
as a hummingbird. Whatever those yolk-yellow

eyes can see through the sifted rain, the pear-
shaped crow just sits there. Through streets
slickened by mist I drive home to that crow.

Cabbage

———————

Diogenes admonished a young courtier,
If you lived on cabbage, you would not
be obliged to flatter the powerful. But

the courtier loathed the stone that dulled
his shovel, and scorned the clod from under
which the earwig blithered. What folly

to dote on your nicknamed pigs, or to cede
a year's dinners to the slow soil and fickle sky.
Well, if you flattered the powerful,

the courtier spat back, *you wouldn't be*
touting cabbages, buried to their necks and born
in rows like slaves. What wish could they dream

fulfilled, those heads without eyes or mouths,
unless it be that the staunch mute will inherit
the scarred earth from the rich and their rarer foods?

———————

Scenic View

From the scorch and poverty, from the cumin and opulence
of the Indian plains, dust gathers and spores convene.
Pollen, insects alive or in desiccate husk,

flecks of grit and commas lost in translation between
one of India's fifteen official languages and another —
all these are lofted by thermals toward the nival

heaven of the Himalayas, where it's so cold the warmth
of a dead insect — its last, gray-embered smidge
of decay — is enough to burn through the onionskin

snow crust an icy, open grave, which will soon
be pillaged by a phalangid spider who knows how
to snatch the remains without dislodging the rim

or becoming the depth, so delicate is the future
at 16,000 feet, where the genetic code burns like a pilot
light in every body, in each of the future's parasites.

Days Beyond Recall

———————

Learned Santayana described himself
as "an ignorant man, almost a poet."
By "poet" I hope he meant neither a career

nor a state of being (*cf.* angel; *cf.* wretch), but
a student of the future and thus of the past.
The older our poet grows (nostalgia being

a dotage), the more past he has to love
and powder and dandle, and so he might use up
his dwindling future like a cake of soap,

or he can turn to that future expectantly,
the way a Jesuit might search his mirror for a skull,
and from the mists of waking and shaving

a skull will blandly greet him. Or he can
smolder along the fuse of his ignorance —
almost a poet, almost a future, almost dead.

———

Caddies' Day, the Country Club,
a Small Town in Ohio

On Mondays even the rich work,
we'd joke around the caddy shack,
though our idea of the rich
was Buick dealers we resented
for their unappeasable daughters.
Mondays the club was closed
except to us, who toiled around
its easy eighteen holes: three hills,
six traps. The water hazard was the pool.
We'd play as slowly as we could,
as if to stretch a day of rest
weeklong. That's any Monday but
the one Bruce Ransome came up
from the bottom of the pool
like a negative rising in a tank,
his body clear, dead, abstract.
Our ignorance lay all around us
like a landscape. So this
is the surface of earth, this loam
so fecund it's almost money,
the top half dredged from Canada
by kindly glaciers, the bottom
ours by blind luck, nature's version

of justice. So this is the first death.
And there I was, green as the sick
and dying elephant in the Babar
book I thought I had outgrown.
That elephant was so wrinkled
he might have drowned over and over,
like a character in a story
whom the author had made unlucky.
The lucky stand in a green stupor
like a beautiful forest. And
their gossip is about how the lucky
link arms, and the living, how the surface
bears us up from Monday to Monday
like a story about persistence,
so that the long work of memory
goes on, its boredom and its courage
and its theology of luck, which
is finally a contest that luck wins.
Do you want my premature stroke?
Do I want your retarded child?
Do you want Bruce Ransome green
in your dowsing arms you can't link
anymore with mine, they're so full

---

of death-rinsed Bruce, or do you want
to lay him down forever,
one long Monday to the next
and to the next one after that,
and let the long week adhere
to your fingers like grime, like matter's
fingerprints, like manual labor,
like an entire life's work?

Dog Life

———————

Scuffed snout, infected ear, ticks like interest
on a loan. Butt of jokes that would, forgive me,
raise hair on a bald dog. Like the one about the baby

so ugly that to get a dog to play with it,
they had to tie a pork chop around the baby's neck.
Or, get this, when you're not working like a dog,

you're dogging it. Yet those staunch workers,
human feet, are casually called dogs, and they're
like miners or men who work in submarines,

hard men who call each other sons of bitches
when they're mad. No wonder it's not loyalty
to dogs that dogs are famous for, since it's men

who've made dogs famous. And don't we understand about having masters, and having food?
Masters are almost good enough for us.

———————

By Heart

_____

Halfway through his 1937 version of "High Society,"
Bechet set aside his phlegmy soprano sax and played
the canonical Alphonse Picou clarinet solo note for note.

Every ventriloquial phrase had Bechet's torque,
as if he were most fundamentally himself when free
from his manic charm and furious invention.

Which came first, style or content? To this trick
question Drs. Xtl and Yrf and Professor Zyzgg
have given honorable gray hours. Style is that rind

of the soul we can persuade to die with us —
no wonder we call it a body of work. Suppose
style is the man or woman, the crumbling reams

of shale, the mango, the brine shrimp, the world
as it is. Is content then what the world isn't?
I don't think so. Content is what style's failed.

_____

Writer-in-Residence

———————

Blowsy geraniums, clay pots stained here
by water and blanched there by Rapid Gro,
a restive cat with the idle in its throat tuned high . . .

No wonder summer is like a series of paintings:
it lacks verbs, though *lacks* is a verb, and *is*.
Time sags like a slack flag. But Shop N Save

has sold summer's last raspberry, and beyond
the topspinning rim of the horizon, dutiful
fall is kneading a squall of work and metabolic

dither. If time is money, teachers are shabbiest
of all the summer rich. The rest of the year we rejoin
the poor we refused to use our educations to escape.

I'm a swarm of pleasantries for my first class.
O syllabus and charisma! But chill is in the air,
and the old rage for work gathers against my indolence.

———————

Free Advice

————————

All day the rain drums its fingers on the roof.
The inner life, we call it — this quarantine,
reading and pacing and feeding the fireplace —

as if it weren't tending our business on its own
like a stealthy heart. The smoke detector bleats
to have its battery replaced. The lobstermen chug

up and down Muscongus Bay to glean their pots.
What's rain to a peeler? Wherever you look,
the inner life is hidden. *Know thyself. If I knew*

myself, I'd run. If you're afraid of loneliness,
don't marry. Nostrum slakes a reader's house,
and the dank woods, too, drip with instruction,

though why we should have thought the woods
wrote English, I've forgot. But now the rain has
lifted, as we say, as if this all were theater.

————————

Minuscule Things

———————

There's a crack in this glass so fine we can't see it,
and in the blue eye of the candleflame's needle
there's a dark fleck, a speck of imperfection

that could contain, like a microchip, an epic
treatise on beauty, except it's in the eye of the beheld.
And at the base of our glass there's nothing

so big as a tiny puddle, but an ooze, a viscous
patina like liquefied tarnish. It's like a text
so short it consists only of the author's signature,

which has to stand, like the future, for what might
have been: a novel, let's say, thick with ambiguous life.
Its hero forgets his goal as he nears it, so that it's

like rain evaporating in the very sight of parched
Saharans on the desert floor. There, by chance, he meets
a thirsty and beautiful woman. What a small world!

———

Aesthetic Distance

In writing, skill is the major share of courage.
From the steamy wheeze
and sleepy, iambic rumble the poet makes,

breathing over the white paper and brown desk,
the poet needs to wrest
a specific rhythm. A little subject matter

helps, though too much can incite a helpless
mastery. Blurred light
on a lawn can lead the apt to the stupid

grandeurs of love, for example, or a beautiful
description of a blue-
fish, the bulldog of the ocean, or a bluefish

fillet marinated in gin and then grilled by
languishing light. . . .
In the meantime, as the puns and toasts disperse

in the August air, as the poet stalls and knots
at the brown desk,
someone is crumpled in a motorcycle crash,

---

another is shot in the Greyhound station and her
brother is named
Man of the Year. The poet has bills to pay and can't

concentrate on poetry until they're paid.
Some days the muse
is at your shoulder like a scolding crow

and some days not. All afternoon the secrecy
of matter seems
to shine from the shrubs outside the poet's

window, the same poet who can no more forget their steady
flare than the poet
can name it. And how would our poet look to the shrubs

if they, like a mute village, could peer back?
Any art has its turpitudes.
Let's imagine, as the poet scribbles a few checks,

the next year or two in the life of the Man of the Year's
mother, and mother
of the Greyhound station's Corpse of the Year.

———

Stale gin and fish fat and burnt charcoal to her are all
the uses of this world.
The poet has $11.62 for the month's last week

and an invitation to a cookout. The mother has ordinary
ashes of bad luck,
for the floods and military police and hotel

fires have spared her, and the diseases that hollow
the body and will
like woodpeckers, and she has had from poverty

and milky slander only twice as much as she could be
strengthened by.
This poem will never be any good, the poet mutters;

the afternoon is beautiful and all are sad.
Our mother is drinking
mediocre sherry and we're making fine distinctions.

The poet trudges to the desk. Insomniac
Sappho sat here,
radiant with desire, and quizzical Horace,

———

and Byron smirking, and oceanic Whitman,
and Emily Dickinson
in a dress whiter than the inside of an oyster shell.

The afternoon was beautiful and the whole
imagined weight
of grief enough to convert a fern to a diamond

in the three hours our poet writes and cancels
and writes some more.
How far must our mother run to escape her grief?

That's aesthetic distance. The poet looks up.
The light on the lawn
is blurred. The bluefish are running, and people

are dying. There's a phrase in the eleventh line
our poet hates.
Love is fierce. The phrase must be changed.

Self-knowledge

High above the slant snow and sludged traffic,
smug as Horace on the Sabine farm and twice
as indolent, I read Horace until the gray is wholly

drained from the afternoon. The docile sheep,
the fire fed by a servant, those jars of Falernian,
for which the occasion is pleasure itself,

maturing in the cellar like negotiable bonds . . .
I could send out for Chinese food. I could
pop a Bud Powell tape into the box. I could

wrap myself in wrath and my oldest coat
and scowl through the slickening streets, looking
for someone to haunt, and who would it be?

I'd know his limp anywhere, his stoic jokes,
that battered coat. The poor, pained, brave
son of a bitch, I'd know him anywhere.

Search for the Perfect Pasta

———————

Little hats, little bow ties, little bridegrooms
with and without grooves, tiny stars, little seashells,
little ribbons, sparrows' tongues, little Cupids,

little rings, tiny pearls, little chickens, tiny worms —
the world shrunk to bite size by gluttony and Italian's
genius for diminuendo: *piccolo, piccolino,* dwindle

and gone. Too small to see, like the exact
discriminations we herded from one hill town
to the next: the tagliatelle were better in Todi.

Replete in our rented car, drilling the dark homeward,
we'd talk in switchbacks up the mountain
about women and marriage, making rueful

contrasts and comparisons, as if we weren't single
by terror, as if marriage were an art and we
the victims of our own high standards for our work.

———————

City Planning

To be above the slough and sewage and mud,
the horseshit, the clang and sparks of horse-
shoes, the blue pennants of car exhaust,

the genial and obscene ruckus of contending
cabbies, the waft of rat- and dog-
luring garbage, the antiphonal tide

of crime and police — who wouldn't desire it?
Not from small space only does a city
grow upward, but also for quiet sleep

and the light for which buildings vie like a gang
of gawky plants. Cars plead their loud torts
in the streets. Rats shinny up the dumbwaiter

ropes like the expectations of the middle class.
Never mind, we'll invent the elevator, broaden
the tax base, and build up. Away we go.

Hope

_____

Beautiful floors and a lively
daughter were all he'd wanted, and then —
that the dear piñata of her head

not loose its bounty, the girl's
father scored the soles of her new shoes
with a pocketknife, that she not slide

nor skid nor turn finally upside-
down on the oak floors he'd sanded
and buffed slick long before she first

gurgled from her crib. Now he's dead
and she's eighty. That's how time
works: it's a tough nut to crack

and then a sapling, then a tree, and
then somebody else's floor long
after we ourselves are planted.

_____

Orthopedic Surgery Ward

───────────

And what else? The rain-beaded cars in rows,
the pale, foreshortened city awash on the gray
horizon, two skeletal poplars, an unslaked sky.

On the bed next to mine, an old man, dying,
drifts on a thermal of morphine. And I, less ill
by far but rancid with boredom, hold my bad

leg numb and still. The days seem like a long
choral breath — some of us breathe easy, some wheeze
and strain, a few are dictated to by machines.

Now the rain, and now the light comes obliquely
from the west. At night the hale lie down, too,
though a few are chosen to watch for us all,

to monitor the machines that monitor the sick
while loneliness, complacent and businesslike,
conducts its brisk, meticulous rounds.

───────

Recovery Room

How bright it would be, I'd been warned.
To my left an old woman keened steadily,
Help me, help me, and steadily a nurse delivered
false and stark balm to her crumpled ear:
You'll be all right. Freshly filleted, we lay

drug-docile on our rolling trays, each boat
becalmed in its slip. I was numb waist-down
to wherever I left off, somewhere between my waist
and Budapest, for I was pointed feet-first east.
I had the responsibility of legs, like tubes

of wet sand, but no sensation from them.
Anyone proud of his brain should try to drag
his body with it before bragging. I had to wait
for my legs and bowels and groin to burn
not with their usual restlessness but

back toward it from anesthetic null. I felt —
if *feel* is the right verb here — like a diver
serving time against the bends. And O
there were eight of us parked parallel
as piano keys against the west wall of that

light-shrill room, and by noon we were seven,
though it took me until I got to the surface
to miss her. Especially if half of me's been trans-
planted by Dr. Flowers, the anesthesiologist,
I'm divided, forgetful. I hated having an equator,

below which my numb bowels stalled and my bladder
dully brimmed. A terrible remedy for these
drug-triggered truancies was "introduced,"
as the night nurse nicely put it, and all
the amber night I seeped into a plastic pouch,

and by dawn, so eager was I to escape, and ever
the good student, I coaxed my bowels to turn
a paltry dowel. Here was proof for all of us:
my legs were mine to flee on once again.
Even a poet can't tell you how death enters

an ear, but an old woman whose grating voice
I hated and whose pain I feared died next to me
while I waited like a lizard for the first fizzles
of sensation from my lower, absent, better half:
and like a truculent champagne,

———

the bottom of my body loosed a few
petulant bubbles, then a few more,
and then. . . . You know the rest.
Soon they let me go home and I did.
Welcome back, somebody said. Back? Back?

Black Box

────────────

Because the cockpit, like the snowy village in a paperweight,
parodies the undomed world outside, and because
even a randomly composed society like Air Florida

flight #7 needs minutes for its meeting, the tape
in the black box slithers and loops with its slow,
urinary hiss like the air-filtering system in a fall-

out shelter. What's normally on the tape? Office life
at 39,000 feet, radio sputter and blab, language
on automatic pilot. Suppose the flight should fail.

Cosseted against impact and armored against fire,
the black box records not time but history. Bad choice.
The most frequent last word on the black box

tape is "Mother." Will this change if we get
more female pilots? Who knows? But here's
the best exchange: "We're going down." "I know."

Leipzig, 1894

We have only one portrait of Bach — that genius,
mule, and rock upon which music built her church —
and that portrait has been painted over, and restored.

I don't know what we thought we'd find,
but we opened his grave. Each clammy sweat bead
on my arms grew colder. Did I think

a mud dove would fly up from his broken grave?
If the body is resurrected, it leaves its bones behind.
To judge from these, he was of medium build.

And all that dirt would have to be shoveled back.
Behind us — for we all faced inward like a random
family at a deathbed — the dark kept its distance.

The lantern flames tossed their heads this way and that.
The harder I listened, the deeper I heard us breathe.
What music, after all, had we disturbed?

Schoolboys with Dog, Winter

It's dark when they scuff off to school.
It's good to trample the thin panes of casual
ice along the track where twice a week

a freight that used to stop here lugs grain
and radiator hoses past us to a larger town.
It's good to cloud the paling mirror

of the dawn sky with your mouthwashed breath,
and to thrash and stamp against the way
you've been overdressed and pudged

into your down jacket like a pastel
sausage, and to be cruel to the cringing
dog and then to thump it and hug it and croon

to it nicknames. At last the pale sun rolls
over the horizon. And look!
The frosted windows of the schoolhouse gleam.

Mail Order Catalogs

———————

Pewter loons, ceramic bunnies, and faux bamboo
are for the suburbs, and bird feeders in Tudor
and saltbox models, and tulips to force in delft.

But in smoky bars in small towns late on week nights,
where the old songs on the jukebox call in
their emotional debts only from habit,

for everyone's derisively broke, and farther out
in the washes and hollows from which men
drive vehicles to town to apply for loans for vehicles,

and from which women must buy a good dress by mail —
loneliness is the product and the customer gets sold to it:
country music, booze, and sunset shot through the cheesecloth

of topsoil powdered as fine in the dusky air as make-up
rich women wear back east. Once this darkening sky
was ocean thousands of feet up, and we were floor.

———

Attention, Shoppers

There's a blue light special in aisle six.
We've mounded toddlers' sneakers higher than desire.
I wanted to expose you, she said, taking off her dress.

At the end of the worm, there's a tunnel.
Long into the night the endless night wends on.
I didn't know what to do, so I did it longer.

Grammar wants to conclude but humans to continue.
In their sturdy shoes they go as far as they can.
Good deeds seldom go long unpunished.

Gold was cheap, and you, you asshole, you bought tires.
Family life, that's what we're selling here.
Alas, parents love their children more than vice versa.

Here's how I'll know: I'll be placid as a lagoon.
It's so hard to describe, it can't be described.
Horse, foot, and artillery, I fought it, and I lost.

Three Vacations

---

1. Mérida, 1969

for Russell Banks

We sat in the courtyard
like landlords and dispatched
teak-colored Manolo
at intervals for Carta Blanca,
and propped idiomatic
little wedges of lime on top
of the bottles like party hats.
O tristes tropiques. Our pretty
wives were sad and so were we.
So this is how one lives when one
is sad, we almost said out loud.
Manolo, we cried, and his tough
feet came skittering across
the blue, rain-streaked tiles.

Travel turned out to be no
anodyne, for we went home.
It was a sort of metaphor,
we now agree, a training
in loss. For if we'd been happy

---

then, as now we often are,
we'd have sat there in Mérida
with its skyline of church spires
and windmills, the latter
looking like big tin dande-
lions from which the fluff
had just been blown by wind
they couldn't resist, and we'd cry
Manolo, and beer would arrive.

2. Spring Training, the Cincinnati Reds, Tampa, 1952

To a boy, it was like *The Iliad* live.
Not tottering on their spikes, the heroes
loped and spat and posed. The fans
seemed older than baseball itself,
which was somehow like family life.
"Is Jennifer coming down this year?"
"No, she has a new beau." And all
would understand, though I was ferally
ignorant and offered my tiny paw
for Ted Kluszewski to shake; his

———

39

liniment-marinated slab of a hand
pumped my matchstick forearm
abstractly and tenderly,
the way one might milk a goat.

Each March the Rosey Reds, mostly
retired, flew south to watch a week
of baseball and trade maxims. *Y'aint
learned to sew till you can rip*,
I once heard twice in half an inning.
Also they would exchange medical news,
more harrowing each year. Lithe
second basemen who can't hit — *How much
you think that twig weighs anyhow?* —
fall back to the minors every spring,
but the veterans of angiograms
and triple bypasses come back
to judge the young and turn their faces
like a stand of sunflowers.

3. Fairbanks, the Summer Solstice, 1983

A curtain of mosquitoes wavered,
as we did, in the unrelenting light.
We'd need to conduct a courtship
without darkness. And we managed,
day and night. Birdsong's a good
substitute for sunrise, and terror
for the dark. Remember how we skimmed
the snaggle-toothed Alaska Range
and then — *Time for some serious nose-
down flying*, our gleeful pilot said —
we drilled 3,000 feet of lumpy air
and landed like a reckless feather?
What good hands we were in:
four of them were ours. *Sometimes*

*you have to buzz the bulldozed
landing strips to startle a dreamy
moose away*, our pilot told his
dreamy rubes. Sometime in the blanched
night Denali had spurned its purdah
of clouds, and so we watched it fill

---

the windshield like the future,
which in the case of rock is like the ages.
Downdrafts and thermals fought not
for our souls but for our vivid bodies.
Remember how those thermals worked?
Faster than any plane could fly or we could fear,
we'd be hiccupped hundreds of feet aloft,
and, white with fear, we loved it.

Liver Cancer

And then, he said, *I knew it was my job*
to go home and wither and die. We found him three
days from success and almost couldn't tell

if the flame melting him was rage or the disease
itself. How could it burn off so much *lebensraum*
between two check-ups six months apart?

Because he was so healthy. In a frail man
cancer would falter and creep. It uses what you are.
What did we talk about? Family life, money,

the obdurate sorrows of childhood.
Not about sex, nor death, those blown fuses.
Suppose that as cells age, they individuate,

like members of a family. One day they've grown
so far into their several futures the kinship taboo
has paled. It won't be long until someone attacks.

Construction

———————

Livid and tiny, all burble and breast milk
with its chalky undertaste, how could you begin
to stack a totter of nouns and verbs? And now

you knit languid and urgent sentences as readily
as you eat or pee. Thick wrists, muddy boots,
straw, and clay: what work the hod-carrying

and wheelbarrowing of speech entailed, though
nothing you can say, even now, bears much
of a load. Much goes unsaid. *Because*, the adamant

child explains. . . . And stops, for the world can be
so dense with meaning, built like a brick shithouse,
that one grows dense as well. Would it surprise

such a child if the skeins of air that wound
in and out of its lungs bore the minute erasures
of dust and the dank evaporations of rain?

———————

Puberty

———————

Remember the way we bore our bodies to the pond
like raccoons with food to wash? Onto the blue,
smooth foil of the gift-wrapped water I slid

my embarrassing self. All the water I knew
was from books. I had read of the surfless Adriatic
and read how the North Atlantic erected by night

its wavering cliffs of fog and cul-de-sacs of ice,
only to turn to the dawn its chill, placid cheek.
But twitch and thrash in my chair as I might,

it was true what the swimming teacher told me:
once you learn how to float, it's almost impossible
to go under. I tried and tried, and so I can tell you

how we greet the news by which we survive: with rage.
A bucolic boy adrift on a Xenia, Ohio, pond?
Not on your life. Like you, I gulped and learned to swim.

———————

Torch Song

——————

From its shifting skin the bay had erased in turn
the diligent scribbles of the lobster boats, the stitches
tacking sailboats made, every glint and blur the sun

had sown on the busy waters. The ride ran reticently
out and chummily back in, and cormorants dove
where herons had plied six hours earlier. At dusk,

the wind stalled and the bay lay glassily bland.
Later, moths convened on the bright windows like recurring
dreams. Who will remember this unless it repeat itself?

Weren't melons sapid and berries taut with sugar?
Didn't the spirit wisp smokily from the rose-gray
embers of the sleeping body? The way it draggled

back at dawn, famished and damp, you'd swear
it had risked your life, and you'd be right
unless you failed to call that exhaustion happiness.

Blue Notes

How often the blues begin early morning.
In the net of waking, on the mesh: bitter dew.
It's as if we'd been watered with nightmares

and these last squibs were the residue,
a few splatters from an evaporated eloquence
we can't reconstruct for all the cocaine

in Bogotá or winter wheat in Montana.
The blues tick in the wrist, even as the body
trudges its earnest portage to the shower.

Fight fire with fire and water with water.
You know that smirk in the blues? It turns out
the joke's on us. Each emotion lusts for its opposite —

which is to say, for itself. Our water music
every morning rains death's old sweet song,
but relentless joy infests the blues all day.

Vasectomy

———

After the vas deferens is cut, the constantly
manufactured sperm cells die into the bloodstream
and the constant body produces antibodies

to kill them. Dozens of feet of coiled wiring
need to be teased out and snipped at the right spot,
and then, local anesthetic winding down, the doc

has to stuff it all back in like a flustered motorist
struggling to refold a road map. But never mind,
you'll fire blanks forever after. At first you may feel

peeled and solitary without your gang of unborn
children, so like the imaginary friends of childhood
and also like those alternate futures you'll never

live out and never relinquish because they're company,
and who'd blame you preferring company to love?
Most of the other animals live in groups we've named

so lavishly we must love them. Lions: a pride.
Foxes: a skulk. Larks: an exaltation. And geese:
a skein in the sky and a gaggle on the ground.

———

Venereal nouns, they're called, for the power Venus
had to provoke allegiances. But the future comes
by subtraction. The list dwindles of people

you'd rather be than you. Nobody in a dream
is dead, so when you wake at 5:00 A.M. to scuffle
across the hall and pee, to lower your umber line

and reel it back in dry, and then to lie back down
and bob like a moored boat two hours more,
you think how if you brought them all — the dead,

the living, the unborn — promiscuously on stage
as if for bows, what a pageant they'd make!
They would. They do. But by then you're back to sleep.

———

Notes

"April in the Berkshires":
The Mr. Forsyth who appears in line 13
of this poem is the one for whom
forsythia was named.

"Herd of Buffalo Crossing the Missouri on Ice":
The poem takes its title from an American
painting I've never seen.

"Hope":
The motto of William of Orange was
"Enterprise does not require hope." The
anecdote of the shoes I took from Eudora
Welty's *One Writer's Beginnings*.

"Three Vacations," part 3:
Denali is the Indian name for what mapmakers
persist in calling Mount McKinley.
